ERNIE

OUT OF CONTROL...

A collection of
sophisticated
literature and fine
art by B. Grace

Ernie is distributed internationally by King Features Syndicate, Inc. For information write King Features Syndicate, Inc., 216 East 45th Street, New York, New York 10017.

ISBN: 0-8362-2123-0

Library of Congress Catalog Card Number: 96-83994

FORWARD →

Hello, folks. I was going to hire somebody famous to write this introduction, but the cheapskates all wanted to get paid. Well, they had their chance to bask in the limelight of this classy book and they blew it! Hey, someday they'll come crawling back!

ERNIE first appeared in February 1988. This is the first substantial *ERNIE* anthology to appear in the United States, although there are several foreign language collections available in Europe. I put together a comic book a few years ago which was pretty good, and in 1990 there was a small trade paperback which is now out of print. But this is the first real American *ERNIE* book. It's got to be a collector's item. I suggest you go out right now and buy two or three more copies. Give one to your mother. When I die they're going to be worth a fortune.

This book contains all of the daily strips that appeared in the U.S. in 1992 and the first few weeks of 1993, plus a few surprises. They are pretty much in the same order in which they originally appeared, although I did move a few around to make the book fit together better. It doesn't really matter. I try to work ten to twenty weeks in front of my deadlines and I seldom publish material in the same order in which it was drawn. I've held some stories for years before I've gotten up the nerve to send them.

For those of you who read *ERNIE* in the newspaper, you know what to expect. For those of you picking up *ERNIE* for the first time in this book, good luck. To help you keep things straight, here's what the major miscreants look like . . .

This is Ernie, except that since this photograph was taken, he shaved off his moustache. He's a bachelor, a college grad (Univ. of Bayonne), and assistant manager of a Mr. Squid franchise.

Doris Husselmeyer is Ernie's squeeze.

Spencer is her brother.

This is Ernie's uncle, Sid Fernwilter, entrepreneur, investor, and perennial treasurer of a benevolent and protective organization known as the Piranha Club.

Arnold Arnoldski is our pubescent 18-year-old.

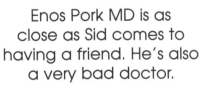

Enos Pork MD is as close as Sid comes to having a friend. He's also a very bad doctor.

Ethel, AKA Effie Munyon, is Ernie's landlady, a poor cook, and Sid's daily free meal ticket.

Earl is Sid's beloved piranha . . . mascot of the Piranha Club.

Mr. Squid is actually a puppet, here worn by. . .

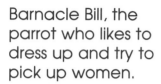

Barnacle Bill, the parrot who likes to dress up and try to pick up women.

Then there's Rev. Bob, Elvis Zimmerman who sells used cars, the criminally insane Wurlitzer brothers, Frau Pork and her mom Mother Packer, Sid's neighbor Henslow, Zerblatt from the planet Grelzak, the last commie Joe Zarinky, and God knows who else. No wonder people can't figure out this strip.

I'll be the first to admit that I don't always produce material that's in the best of taste. That's unfortunate for me because the comic section is the last bastion of wholesomeness in most newspapers, and most features editors mean to keep it that way. That's why my editor and his toadies at King Features try to keep me in line. Virtually everything I draw has to go through the syndicate V.P. Consequently we're always altering dialogue, changing panels and sometimes completely dropping strips. There have been cases where we've actually killed or indefinitely postponed entire stories. The constant editing has had a constrictive effect on my work. Over the years I've become like a lab rat in a shock box. I've learned to censor

myself in advance to cut back on the redraws and lost time. But occasionally I'll draw up a good gag and send it in just to shock my editor.

I'm not really complaining. My editor is a perfect example of a necessary evil. Several years ago, I did a story about falling cows in which I made a few political jokes. I immediately lost fifteen newspapers. We had to circle the wagons and pull four weeks of questionable dailies, two weeks of which were never published in this country. A similar thing happened recently when a publisher objected to my story about Arnold's sister. During the subsequent barracuda story we were forced to alter several strips and kill three outright, including the story's ending.

In this book I've restored the original dialogue as best I could, and I've used the original unaltered drawings. In a few places I've added notes on some of the alterations. In the back there's a short appendix with some examples of strips which have been nixed by my editor or, in some cases, by me. Some are politically incorrect, some are considered mean spirited, and some are just plain gross. Nevertheless, I'm sure you will consider at least some of them to be absolutely innocuous.

So here you go. The book you've all been asking for . . . or dreading. If you like it you can write to me at PO Box 66, Oakton, Virginia 22124, or e-mail me at Piranhaclb@aol.com. And if you really want the latest poop, check out my web site at http://www.piranhaclub.com.

QUACKO, THE HUMAN DUCK.

I have a recurring dream that I'm engaged to be married to a woman who has a neatly trimmed thick black beard. I reason (in my dream) that it's not unusual for women to have beards, but deep down there is a nagging suspicion that all is not as it should be. It's the same feeling I get when I dream that I'm out in public without my pants. I'm sure it's all very Freudian.

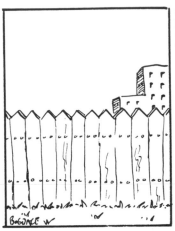

This last strip never appeared in print. My editor thought it might be offensive to Asians. I've never been in a Chinese restaurant yet that didn't serve duck. The preceding strip was its replacement.

THE LAST COMMIE...

is one of the few characters in *ERNIE* who is based entirely on an actual living human being. The real "Joe Zarinky"—I altered his name a little bit—was and still is a marvelous, brilliant, yet some-what eccentric chap. He was a friend of mine whom I knew back in the '70s. His parents had been active in the labor move-ment. He, himself, was politically active and as a young man was a victim of McCarthyism. He even had a case argued before the Supreme Court. (He lost.) When he retired he fulfilled his life-long dream by going back to graduate school and earning his doctorate in political science. He finally became a Ph.D. commie. The next week Gorbachev was out, Yeltsin was in, and the commie job market was in shambles.

SID, A BUNCH OF US ON THE BLOCK ARE GETTING TOGETHER AND FORMING A NEIGHBORHOOD WATCH!

SID'S NEXT-DOOR NEIGHBOR

WE'LL KEEP AN EYE ON EACH OTHERS' HOUSES... LOOK OUT FOR SUSPICIOUS CHARACTERS... IF WE SEE SOMETHING WE'LL CALL THE POLICE!

WE FIGURE IF WE GET TOGETHER ON THIS WE CAN GET RID OF SOME OF THE CRIME IN THE NEIGHBORHOOD!

AND YOU WANT ME TO JOIN

WE WANT YOU TO MOVE

BOORACE

BOY, THAT HENSLOW REALLY BURNS ME UP!

HOW COME?

BERACE

HE STARTED A NEIGHBORHOOD WATCH! THEY KEEP A LOOK-OUT FOR SUSPICIOUS CHARACTERS

SOUNDS GOOD TO ME

WHENEVER THEY SPOT ONE, THEY PUT HIM UNDER CONSTANT SURVEILLANCE TO MAKE SURE HE DOESN'T TRY ANYTHING

WHAT'S WRONG WITH THAT?

FOR CRYIN' OUT LOUD GIVE IT A BREAK!

MRS. HOROWITZ, WATCH SECTOR 2 - AND STAY ALERT! THERE'S BEEN LOTS OF MURDERS AND MUGGINGS THERE LATELY!

OK

EL RANCHO ST. NEIGHBORHOOD WATCH ASS'N

MR. HAIRWIG, KEEP AN EYE ON SECTOR 3 - WE'VE HAD QUITE A FEW MAFIA HITS, SERIAL KILLERS AND MAJOR DRUG TRANSACTIONS DOWN THERE!

YESSIR

THE REST OF YOU BETTER COME WITH ME!

REMEMBER, MEN, THERE'S STRENGTH IN NUMBERS!

G'WAN BEAT IT!

BERACE

ISN'T THIS NEIGHBOR-HOOD WATCH GETTING ON YOUR NERVES?

I'LL SAY! THANK GOD IT'S ALMOST EIGHT O'CLOCK!

FINALLY!

WHAT HAPPENS AT EIGHT O'CLOCK?

THAT'S WHEN MRS. BOLINSKI DOWN THE STREET TAKES HER SHOWER

BEING WATCHED 24 HOURS A DAY WOULD DRIVE ME UP THE WALL!

IT'S NOT SO BAD

YOU DON'T MIND?

NOT SINCE I HIRED MY ASSISTANT

LARGE BUTTER POPCORN AND A BOX OF JUJUBEES

I DON'T HAVE TIME TO COOK TONIGHT, SO I BOUGHT SOME FROZEN TV DINNERS

FROZEN DINNERS?!

I GOT AN ENCHILADA DINNER, A MEAT LOAF DINNER AND A CHICKEN TERIYAKI... WHAT DO YOU WANT

ALL THREE!

ALL I HAVE TO DO IS COOK THEM FOR 35 MINUTES!

IT'S PRETTY HARD TO SCREW UP A TV DINNER!

GEE....MAYBE I SHOULDN'T HAVE BOILED THEM ALL IN THE SAME POT

35

40

In the published version Agent Rodriguez was wearing a much less revealing gown. I also slipped and mentioned the real Joe Zarinky's first name in the first panel of the first strip above.

ZERBLATT

I'LL TRY TO HAVE HIM HOME BY MIDNIGHT

No, I have never been abducted by aliens. I can't for the life of me figure out why not. If they'd want **anybody** you'd think they'd want **me**. I ought to join that bunch of loonies that go out in the Arizona desert in the middle of the night with binoculars and signs painted on the top of their heads that say "TAKE **ME**." When I was a kid my friend Larry Jerome's mother got chased by a flying saucer, but she got away. That's as near as I've ever come to a close encounter. Unless you count my first wife.

MEANWHILE, OVER AT THE GINSU PALACE...

SLICE WAK HAK WAK

TOSS

HI-YAH!

SLICE STAB WOUND

SSSS

EEEEEEEEE

CUT MAIM WHAK

BETTER GIVE HIM A REAL BIG TIP!

PANT PANT PANT

BOINGGGG

I NEED TO GET A DRIVER'S LICENSE

OK — HOLD THIS AND FACE THE CAMERA

FLASH

27261582

NOW TURN SIDEWAYS

FLASH

27261582

IT SAVES TIME LATER

ERNIE — WHEN WE... I MEAN IF WE GET MARRIED, HOW MANY KIDS DO YOU WANT TO HAVE?

OH... TEN OR TWELVE MINIMUM!

MAN ON FIRST... ONE OUT

IF WE DIDN'T HAVE AT LEAST TWELVE CHILDREN, I'D BE VERY BITTERLY DISAPPOINTED!

HERE'S THE PITCH...

STRIKE THREE

DORIS IS GREAT... BUT EVERY SO OFTEN YOU HAVE TO COOL HER JETS

WE HAVE A VERY NICE **ALFREDO SAUCE**, WE HAVE A **MARINARA SAUCE** WITH A TOUCH OF **GARLIC**, OR WE HAVE A **DELICIOUS** FRESH BASIL PESTO.

WHAT WOULD YOU LIKE ON YOUR LINGUINI, SPENCER?

BZZZZ BZZZ

JELLY

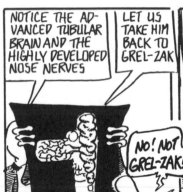

THIS NEBLON WALKS INTO A ZEBBERBLUN AND ASKS FOR A NERBNORG... THE FLUMMAK SAYS "DO YOU WANT THAT WITH A BUNTFIG?"

THE NEBLON SAYS "ONLY IF IT COMES WITH A NORZNIK"

HAH!

HA HA HA HA HA HOO HOO HA HA HIK HIK HUK HAK HAK HUK HIK HAK YAK HIK HAK

IT'S NOT THE ≋GASP≋ JOKE! IT'S ≋WHEEZE≋ THE WAY YOU TELL IT!

BOGRACE

WHA?!!...

THIS IS ZERBLATT

SLURP

BOGRACE

WHERE'S HE FROM?!

I HAVE TRAVELLED THROUGH TIME AND SPACE... THROUGH DIMENSIONS OF LIGHT AND DARKNESS...

I HAVE DANCED UPON THE NEBULAE AND BEEN ONE WITH THE COSMOS...

I HAVE SPANNED THE EONS... I HAVE...

OH

HE'S FROM CALIFORNIA

HE CAN'T DRINK... HE'S FROM CALIFORNIA

WHO CAN'T DRINK?!

BOGRACE

BACK ON GREL-ZAK I'VE BEEN KNOWN TO DOWN TWO DOZEN NEBLONIAN FIZZES BEFORE MY FIRST TRIP TO THE CAN!...

BIG DEAL!...

GREL-ZAKIAN DRINKS DON'T CONTAIN ALCOHOL!

WHAT THE HECK IS THE ACTIVE INGREDIENT IN A NEBLONIAN FIZZ?

PRUNE JUICE

65

HEY FOLKS, JUST KIDDING!

I SURE HATE TO LEAVE THAT OLD BUILDING! AT LEAST WE'LL GET SOMETHING FOR THE PLUMBING AND THE LIGHT FIXTURES!

AND THE WOOD!

RUMBLE

I MEAN THE BEAMS HAVE GOT TO BE WORTH AT LEAST A COUPLE HUNDRED!

WELL, WE LOST THE LODGE... NOW WHAT DO WE DO?!

NOBODY IN THEIR RIGHT MIND IS GOING TO RENT A BUILDING TO THE PIRANHA CLUB!

I KNOW A PLACE...

BUT IT'LL COST US FIFTY BUCKS A NIGHT

THAT'S FIVE BUCKS APIECE

I MOVE WE PUT THE SLOT MACHINES IN THE KITCHEN...

WHAT'S GOING ON IN HERE?!!

NO PIRANHA CLUB MEETINGS IN MY APARTMENT!!

OUT!! OUT!! OUT!! OUT!!

OK, ERNIE-WELL GO....

BUT PLEASE... JUST GIVE US FIVE MINUTES TO FINISH UP?

WELL...

OK.

HOW'S IT GOING?

ONE MORE FAUCET

CREAK

One evening my wife and I were dining with Joe D'Angelo, who is president of the syndicate, and his charming wife, Marcia. She sadly confided to Frau Grace that whereas Joe had often appeared in the comics, she had never. She got her wish . . . .

In the published version it was pointed out that Mrs. D'Angelo's weapon of self-destruction was a butter knife.

72

The moose milking story was inspired by the 1992 Winter Olympics. If you recall, many Americans were outraged because our hockey team was mugged by the Swedes. I've been to Sweden on several occasions. My first visit there was the inspiration for the original moose story which appeared a year or so before this one. I had to replace two strips in this sequence. The first was the one about the male rhinoceros. Sure, there are people with dirty minds who would read more into this than was intended. It's a shame because it's a good gag. The second was the ending of the story in which the Virgin Islands wins the gold. Here, of course, we were worried about racial sensitivity. But it's like the Jamaican bobsled team. So what if there aren't too many moose on Tortola. Athletes of African descent win almost all the medals anyway. I was smart, though. I used the same gag on both the replacement strips. I'm surprised I didn't catch it on cruelty to animals.

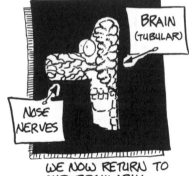

79

LOVE AMONG THE LOWER VERTEBRATES

When I was Arnold's age I was thankful for anyone who would go out with me. I still would be today if it weren't for Frau Grace . . . I think I like this particular little story better than any other I've ever done. Of course in the published version my editor changed "Michael Jackson" and "his monkey" to "Captain Kangaroo" and "Mr. Moose," and "Burt" and "Loni" to "Garry Trudeau" and "Jane Pauley." The reference to "livestock" went out the window like a bat out of heck. (Something about lawsuits. To put the record straight, I'm positive Burt has never dated barnyard animals of any sort.) I changed "guacamole" to "pretzels" on my own. So much more tasteful, don't you think?

"DEAR MR. ARNOLDSKI, YOU ARE **ALREADY A WINNER!** YOU HAVE **ALREADY** GUARANTEED, DEFINITELY WON EITHER A **1992 ROLLS-ROYCE SILVER GHOST** OR A TERRIFIC AJAX TWO MAN STYROFOAM FISHING BOAT. **JUST RETURN** THE ENCLOSED..."

FORGET THAT!

SMART MOVE

YEAH...

...WITH MY LUCK I PROBABLY WON THE ROLLS...

AND I DON'T HAVE A DRIVER'S LICENSE.

MEANWHILE, THE PROLONGED RECESSION IS TAKING IT'S TOLL...

SORRY, FELDMAN YOU'RE BEING **REPLACED** BY A CHIP!

MICRO?

POTATO

TA-TA

EMPLOYERS CAN **PICK** AND **CHOOSE** AMONG JOB APPLICANTS...

WHAT DO YOU KNOW ABOUT **RECOMBINANT** DNA?

DISHWASHER WANTED

SOME ARE BEING **DRIVEN** TO **DESPERATE EXTREMES**!

EVEN PEOPLE WITH **JOBS** ARE FINDING IT **HARD** TO **MAKE ENDS MEET**!

HOW MUCH?

$2.63

YES, FOLKS, THE **INFAMOUS WURLITZER BROTHERS** ARE HAVING A HARD TIME MAKING **ENDS MEET**!...

GEE...

BAYONNE'S MOST CUNNING CRIMINALS

HOW MUCH DID WE MAKE LAST WEEK?

$2.63

IT HURTS MY PRIDE, ED... BUT THERE'S ONLY ONE THING WE CAN DO!

OCCUPATION?

MUGGER

UNEMPLOYMENT COMPENSATION

HEY! THANK GOD FOR OUR SOCIAL SAFETY NET!

HOW MUCH?

$2.63

YES, THE WURLITZER BROS. HAVE BEEN HARD HIT BY THE **SAGGING ECONOMY**!

WHEN WAS YOUR LAST JOB?

FRIDAY

WHAT DID YOU MAKE?

$2.63

WRITE WRITE

UNEMPLOYMENT CLAIMS (FORM A LINE)

$2.63

WHY THAT'S FAR BELOW **MINIMUM WAGE**!

UNEMPLOYMENT CLAIMS (LINE UP)

CHEAPSKATE!

BOOM

YES, FOLKS, IF IT WEREN'T FOR OUR **CRIMINAL JUSTICE SYSTEM**, WE'D REALLY BE IN DEEP HOOEY!

DEAR FOLKS—AS YOU KNOW, FROM TIME TO TIME THIS SPACE IS DONATED TO WORTHWHILE CAUSES. TODAY, MR. PACKER OF THE A.S.P.C.A.

THANK YOU DR. GRACE

FRIENDS, THE A.S.P.C.A. DESPERATELY NEEDS YOUR HELP! WHY, WE CAN'T EVEN SIT DOWN TO LUNCH WITHOUT SOME NOSEY BUSY-BODY RAISING A BIG FUSS!...

PLEASE SEND YOUR GENEROUS CHECK OR MONEY ORDER TO THE AMERICAN SOCIOPATHIC CANNIBALS ASSOCIATION, P.O. BOX...

THUMP!! THUMP!!

URK

SORRY, FOLKS — HE FOOLED ME, TOO! — B. GRACE

ASK DR. PORK

ENOS PORK, M.D.
EYES, EARS, NOSE AND THROAT
(BRAIN SURGERY BY APPOINTMENT)

DOCTOR—IT HURTS WHEN MY WIFE DOES THIS

DIAGNOSIS...

TENNIS ELBOW

KLANG! KLANG! KLANG! KLANG!

DUM DUM DUM DUM DUM DUM DUM DUM...

AAAIIEEE SPLURT CHOMP! GURGLE

BURP

JAWS

This story about male bonding was suggested by Bill Hinds of *Tank McNamara* fame.

I had to redraw the dog here and put in a sign with an arrow that said "fleas." My editor thought it looked like the dog was masturbating. You know where his mind is.

WHY RELATIVES SHOULDN'T MARRY

This is the sort of thing that gets me in hot water at the newspapers. I know it's as hard for you to believe as it is for me, but some people actually think I'm sexist! I find it incredible. There's no one less biased than I am. I treat everybody with the same lack of respect—men, women, teenagers, animals, vegetables . . . I seriously believe that satirizing one sex exclusive of the other is the height of sexism. I can't understand why the same people who could care less about how I ridicule Arnold blow a gasket when I create Arnold's sister in his image . . . And yes, my mother and father were cousins.

108

FOLKS, YESTERDAY I ANNOUNCED THAT HENCEFORTH "ERNIE" WOULD BE SPONSORED BY ED'S SEPTIC TANK CLEANING SERVICE...

ME AGAIN

THIS MORNING, **ABRUPTLY** AND **WITHOUT JUST CAUSE,** ED'S SEPTIC TANK CLEANING SERVICE **CANCELLED** IT'S CORPORATE SPONSORSHIP!

WHY DID THEY DO IT? **HEY!** DON'T ASK **ME!** I JUST **WORK** HERE! FOR NO REASON AT **ALL,** THEY JUST **CANCELLED!!**

THE STRIP WAS HURTING OUR IMAGE

MEANWHILE, FAMOUS "ERNIE" CARTOONIST, BoGRACE IS STILL SEARCHING FOR A SPONSOR...

RCA?

FORD?

GM?...

DITTO

SAID ERNIE'S TOO LOW BROW

ME

MY SECRETARY

PREPARATION 'H'?

ODOR EATERS?

COMPOUND 'W'?

SAID ERNIE DIDN'T HAVE ENOUGH CLASS

TOO SLEAZY

ERNIE'S NOT FIT TO LINE A BIRD CAGE

SLEAZY...

NOT FIT TO LINE A BIRD CAGE...

HMMM...

TAP TAP

HELLO? IS THIS THE NATIONAL ENDOWMENT FOR THE ARTS?

AS YOU KNOW, YESTERDAY I SAW FIT TO TERMINATE MY ADVERTISING CONTRACT WITH **ED'S SEPTIC TANK CLEANING SERVICE** IT WAS A **SLEAZY PRODUCT,** AND I'M GLAD THEY'RE GONE!

GUESS WHO

TODAY I AM PROUD TO BE ASSOCIATED WITH A **BRAND NEW SPONSOR!**...

WHICH, I MIGHT ADD, HAS A LITTLE MORE **CLASS** AND **DIGNITY** THAN THAT LAST **SKUZZY** PRODUCT!

IT'S THE NEW...

WEED-O-MATIC®

NOSE HAIR REMOVAL SYSTEM

BUY ONE TODAY!!

ZZZ

WE NOW JOIN OUR PROGRAM ALREADY IN PROGRESS...

ARNOLD! HOW DID YOU GET A CHICKEN UP YOUR NOSE?

VASELINE

AS YOU RECALL, YESTERDAY ARNOLD HAD A **CHICKEN** STUCK IN HIS **NOSE**...

HMMMM

TAP TAP

B.GRACE

WHY NOT TRY THE NEW **WEED-O-MATIC®** NOSE HAIR REMOVAL SYSTEM?

PERHAPS IT ALSO WORKS ON CHICKENS!

BZZZZZZZ

AH. I CAN BREATHE AGAIN

WEED-O-MATIC®! —NOW AT K-MART

NOW WHAT

PLEASE

WE WILL RETURN IN A MOMENT

WHAT IS THE ESSENCE OF MAN?... STRONG... CONFIDENT...

AND HE DOESN'T HAVE A BUNCH OF NOSE HAIRS STICKING OUT OF HIS CONK

WEED-O-MATIC®

NOSE HAIR REMOVAL SYSTEM

AND NOW BACK TO **ERNIE!**...

LIRK

B.GRACE

I REGRET TO SAY THAT TWO DAYS AGO IN PEORIA, A WEED-O-MATIC® NOSE HAIR REMOVER GOT STUCK IN FAST FORWARD AND REMOVED SOME GUY'S MEDULLA OBLONGATA...

AS A RESULT, ERNIE NO LONGER HAS A SPONSOR!... BUT WILL ERNIE DISAPPEAR FROM THE COMIC PAGES? **NO WAY!**

WHY?..

B.GRACE

BECAUSE PEOPLE WHO READ ERNIE ARE **INTELLIGENT! SOPHISTICATED!** AND THEY RECOGNIZE THE VALUE OF **QUALITY ILLUSTRATED LITERATURE!!**...

RIGHT LYNN?!...

YES, BUD!

VOLUNTEERS ARE WAITING FOR YOUR CALL NOW, SO PICK UP THAT PHONE AND MAKE THAT PLEDGE TODAY

1-800-555-1212

BEFORE WE RETURN TO "ERNIE", FOLKS, LET'S TAKE ONE MORE LOOK AT OUR TOTE BOARD!

PLEDGE NOW! 1-800-555-1212

PLEDGED | GOAL
$ 12 | $65,000

MOI →

1-800-555-1212

IN THE SECOND ACT HE TAKES OFF THE BANANA AND PLAYS "THE GIRL FROM IPANEMA" ON HIS LIPS

PLEDGED | GOAL
$ 0 | $65,000

THE GUY READ THAT LAST PANEL THEN CALLED BACK AND CANCELLED HIS PLEDGE

BGRACE

1-800-555-1212

MY NAME'S YVONNE—I WORK FOR MONROE'S INSURANCE COMPANY

AND A PRETTY GIRL LIKE YOU CAME DOWN HERE JUST TO HELP RAISE MONEY FOR PUBLIC COMICS! GREAT!

RIGHT, CATHY?

RIGHT, BUDDY! AND LOOK WHAT YOU GET WHEN YOU PLEDGE $65!...

PAVAROTTI SINGS THE BLUES! ON COMPACT DISC!

RIGHT, JOHNNY?

THAT'S RIGHT, CATHY! GREAT SONGS LIKE "GIMMIE A PIG'S FOOT AND A BUCKET OF BEER" AND "I WANNA BE YOUR BACK DOOR MAN" AS ONLY PAVAROTTI CAN SING THEM!

BGRACE

BACK TO YOU, BUD

MR. ERWIN SMOOT OF BISMARK NORTH DAKOTA HAS ISSUED A CHALLENGE FOLKS!...

IF WE CAN RAISE $100 BEFORE THE NEXT PLEDGE BREAK, MR. SMOOT WILL MATCH IT!

1-800-555-1212

THAT'S $100 BEFORE OUR NEXT PLEDGE BREAK! I KNOW WE CAN DO IT!

OK—LET'S GO BACK TO "ERNIE"!

YAWN

PLEDGED | GOAL
$ | $100

1-800-555-1212

GOOD NEWS! I THINK WE CAN SAVE YOUR FOOT

GEE, MR. SMOOT! WHILE WE WERE GONE THE PHONES RANG LIKE CRAZY! YOU CAN SEND IN THAT HUNDRED DOLLARS NOW!

SNORE

YAWN

ZZZZ

PLEDGED | GOAL
$4,000 | $100

BGRACE

TODAY'S PHONE VOLUNTEERS FINKED OUT, FOLKS... BUT EVERYTHING'S GOING TO BE OK! THANK GOD MY MOTHER CAME DOWN TO KEEP OUR PLEDGE DRIVE GOING AND...

RING

1-800-555-1212

HELLO, PUBLIC COMIC STRIP... YES... CHICAGO? REALLY? WHAT A COINCIDENCE! I USED TO KNOW...

1-800-555-1212

A LADY FROM CHICAGO! HER NAME WAS LILLY OR MAYBE IT WAS FLORENCE! SHE CANNED TOMATOES BUT THEY DON'T HAVE TOMATOES IN FLORIDA LIKE NORTHERN TOMATOES OF COURSE IT'S COLD IN

1-800-555-1212

NEW JERSEY THE HUMIDITY ISN'T BAD MY LEG DOESN'T ACHE AND THERES OPRAH AND DONAHOO DID YOU SEE THAT WOMAN LAST WEEK SHE WAS MARRIED TO THE HOMICIDAL LUNATIC YAK YAK YAK YAK YA KYAKY YAK..

MAAAA!

1-800-555-1212

THERE'S ONLY A FEW PANELS LEFT IN OUR MEMBERSHIP DRIVE, FOLKS, SO PLEASE PLEASE CALL 1-800-555-1212 NOW! MAKE YOUR PLEDGE! SUPPORT P.C.S.

SNORE

PUBLIC COMIC STRIPS

1-800-555-1212

PLEDGED   GOAL
$ 14 $ 65,000

SKRANXXX

YAWN

1-800-555-1212

WHY, MELL?! WHY HAVEN'T WE GOTTEN ANY CALLS?!

BEE BEE BEE BEE

1-800-555-1212

BECAUSE THAT'S THE NUMBER FOR LONG DISTANCE TOLL FREE INFORMATION

1-800-555-1212

CAN YOU DO ANYTHING ABOUT THIS BIRTHMARK?

HOW LONG HAVE YOU HAD IT?

I NEVER SAW HIM AGAIN.

YOU GOT TO SAVE ME, ERNIE!

WORRY WOE MISERY

MY OLD COLLEGE GIRLFRIEND'S BACK IN TOWN AND SHE'S OUT TO GET ME...

I GOT AWAY ONCE BUT IT WON'T HAPPEN AGAIN...

SOB WHIMPER HELP ME HELP ME

IF ONLY... IF ONLY... IF ONLY...

IF ONLY YOU WERE ALREADY MARRIED

DON'T WORRY, ERNIE! IT'LL GROW BACK!

THE SECRET OF MAKEUP IS IT EMPHASIZES YOUR GOOD FEATURES AND DRAWS ATTENTION AWAY FROM YOUR LESS ATTRACTIVE FEATURES

PFF PFF

POFF POFF POFF POFF

WHAT ARE MY GOOD FEATURES?

COMPARED TO YOUR NOSE...

EVERYTHING

WHAM WHAM WHAM WHAM

IF YOU DON'T WANT PEOPLE TO NOTICE YOUR NOSE WE HAVE TO EMPHASIZE YOUR OTHER FEATURES!

BRIGHT CRIMSON LIPSTICK...

A DELICATE RUBY BLUSH!...

...WITH PINK AND ORANGE UNDERTONES...

BRIGHT TURQUOISE EYE SHADOW...

MIDNIGHT BLUE LINER...

IT'S LIKE PLANTING PETUNIAS AROUND A NUCLEAR POWER PLANT

Of course I love the Stooges, as if you couldn't guess.

In the third strip above we changed "He doesn't know anything about *sex*" to "anything about *the ways of love*." The punch line of this very last cartoon was too naughty even for this book.

APPENDIX

Here are a few that never made the cut. The first one is the ending of the barracuda story which appeared in the summer of 1995. Now, I can see how this particular brand of humor might offend some people. But, heck, it's a mother-in-law joke! What do you expect? The second one was nixed by the syndicate (I later substituted Ernie for the lady and they let it by.). A few months later I went up to New York, and they had it blown up to six feet long and turned into wallpaper for their lobby. Go figure. How about the squid-burger gag! They were worried about the Bulimic Anti-Defamation League. The open-hole-nose-flute gag I didn't even bother to submit. Hey, I got class!